Well-Being

FOR

DUMMIES

Compliments of REAL *Powered by* Humana

WILEY

Wiley Publishing, Inc.

Well-Being For Dummies®

Published by
Wiley Publishing, Inc.
111 River St.
Hoboken, NJ 07030-5774
www.wiley.com

For general information on our other products and services, please contact our Customer Care Department within the U.S. at 877-762-2974, outside the U.S. at 317-572-3993, or fax 317-572-4002.

For technical support, please visit www.wiley.com/techsupport.

Wiley also publishes its books in a variety of electronic formats. Some content that appears in print may not be available in electronic books.

ISBN: 978-0-470-63896-5

Manufactured in the United States of America

10 9 8 7 6 5 4 3 2 1

Publisher's Acknowledgments

Project Editor: Elizabeth Kuball

Composition Services: Indianapolis Composition Services Department

Cover Photos: ©iStockphoto.com/Daniel Bendjy

WILEY

Table of Contents

Introduction

*W*hen you're a kid, the last thing you think about is
well-being. You just take for granted that you'll always
be healthy and happy and have enough money and support.
But as you get older, you realize that these things don't magically appear, and they don't magically stay with you forever.
Instead, you have to work on being well in all areas of your
life, and the first step toward doing that is being informed.

In this book, REAL *Powered by* Humana helps you take charge
of four key areas of well-being — physical, mental, financial,
and social. Each chapter includes helpful tips and expert
advice and is easy to understand, helping you attain well-
being in all areas of your life. It's never too late to get started!

About This Book

Well-Being For Dummies is all about empowering you to take
charge of your well-being and finding a starting point for a
healthier and happier life. It's divided into four chapters that
you can read in succession, like a good novel, or flip to a specific section to find answers to the questions you have today.
Either way, you'll gain the knowledge you need to head into
your future at your best — physically, mentally, financially,
and socially.

Icons Used in This Book

We use icons in the margins throughout this book to draw
your attention to points that are especially valuable or important. Here's what each icon means:

When we tell you something that can save you time or money
or just make your life a little easier, we mark it with this icon.

You don't have to commit this book to memory any more than you have to memorize the dictionary to make use of it. But when we tell you something that's so important that you really *should* remember it, we flag it with this icon.

Life is full of pitfalls and quicksand, but you don't have to fall in. If you heed the warnings marked with this icon, you can sidestep the problems.

Where to Go from Here

Let curiosity be your guide. If you want more information on getting and staying fit, Chapter 1 is for you. If you're looking for ways to reduce stress and attain happiness, turn to Chapter 2. If you want to get your financial life in order, make Chapter 3 your destination. And if you want new ways to connect with your family and friends, Chapter 4 is for you.

Visit www.realforme.com for more information, expert advice and tools that delve deeper into the topics covered in this book. You can also participate in discussions and learn about other issues that are important to you.

Chapter 1

Physical Well-Being: Use It or Lose It

*R*emember the old adage "Without your health, you have nothing"? We're here to tell you that's true. Don't believe us? Here are some benefits of maintaining physical health:

✔ You get stronger, feel fitter, and have more energy.

✔ You control your weight better.

✔ You build and maintain healthy bones, muscles, and joints.

✔ You promote your psychological well-being and reduce feelings of depression and anxiety. (Yep, physical well-being affects mental well-being.)

✔ You reduce your risk of developing high blood pressure.

✔ You reduce your risk of developing colon cancer.

✔ You reduce your risk of dying prematurely (especially from heart disease).

When you're physically fit, you invite overall good health to visit and stay with you a long time. Your mood will improve and you'll feel better about yourself — developments that will impact all areas of your life and overall well-being.

And the best news of all: It's never too late to get started. Even if you and your couch are so intimately acquainted that the cushions have molded to the shape of your body, you can turn things around! And you don't have to overhaul your entire life — you can take small steps that make a huge impact.

In this chapter, we fill you in on everything from weight and nutrition to exercise and sleep.

Winning the Battle of the Bulge

As people grow older, it's common for their weight to creep up. It starts with 5 pounds at the holidays that you don't take off by spring, and it continues with another 5 pounds the next holiday season. Before you know it, you're 10, 15, or 20 pounds overweight.

Being just "a little bit overweight" doesn't mean that you can sit back and feel safe from the serious health concerns associated with being overweight. Even if you're just a little overweight, you are just that — over your healthy weight — and you should try to get down to a healthier number.

The following sections highlight how that extra weight can increase the chance of creating serious symptoms and ways you can get rid of it by counting calories and controlling the urge to overeat.

More than the number on the scale

Your weight is easy to measure: Just hop on a scale and — presto! — you know what you weigh. But weight isn't necessarily the best indicator of how healthy you are. One fitness-scale method that you may hear more about these days is called the *body mass index* (BMI). Physicians and researchers who study obesity find the BMI to be their measurement of choice. BMI uses a mathematical formula that takes into account a person's height and weight.

You can find your BMI, as well as information on what a healthy BMI is, at www.nhlbisupport.com/bmi.

Eyeing the effects of being overweight

The majority of researchers feel that being overweight shares the same health risks as being obese. It's easy to ignore a little extra weight, especially in today's society, and especially if you're the thinnest one in your family or in your circle of friends. But this tendency can give you a false sense of comfort that can be dangerous to your health.

Approximately 30 illnesses and diseases are linked to being overweight. The following represent only a handful of these medical conditions:

- ✔ **Arthritis:** Losing just 10 to 15 pounds is likely to relieve symptoms of arthritis like pain, stiffness, and loss of mobility of the hands, hips, back, and knees.

- ✔ **Cardiovascular disease:** Weight loss helps blood lipid levels by lowering triglycerides and LDL (lousy) cholesterol and increasing HDL (healthy) cholesterol. Losing weight decreases your risk for heart disease.

- ✔ **Diabetes:** If you're overweight, losing as little as 5 percent of your body weight can reduce your high blood sugar.

- ✔ **High blood pressure:** More than 75 percent of high blood pressure cases are reported to be directly attributed to being overweight, and if you lose weight, you're taking an important step toward getting your blood pressure under control.

- ✔ **Sleep apnea:** Obesity is the largest risk factor for developing *sleep apnea,* a condition in which people temporarily stop breathing while they're asleep. Lose weight and you'll lower your risk of developing this condition.

- ✔ **Strokes:** High cholesterol doesn't just affect your heart. People who are overweight increase their risk of *ischemic stroke* (caused by fatty deposits that obstruct blood vessels to the brain). If you lose weight and get your blood lipid levels where they should be, you'll reduce your risk of stroke.

We still haven't convinced you? Consider the following facts:

- ✔ National Cancer Institute experts concluded that obesity is associated with cancers of the colon, breast (post-menopausal), endometrium (the lining of the uterus), kidney, and esophagus.

- ✔ Forty-two percent of those diagnosed with breast and colon cancers are obese.

- ✔ Of all gallbladder surgery, 30 percent is related to obesity.

The good news is that being over your ideal weight isn't a disease without a cure — it's a condition with multiple cures. Achieving a healthy weight is attainable if you start by paying attention to calories, taming your urge to overeat, and incorporating regular exercise.

Counting calories

You need a certain number of calories each day based on the amount of energy you burn. And the amount of energy you burn is determined by your metabolism, your weight, and your activity level.

Regardless of your diet, if you take in more calories than you need, you gain weight. In fact, if you consume 3,500 more calories per week than you need, you gain 1 pound. If you want to lose 1 pound, the reverse is also true — you need to consume 3,500 fewer calories per week or burn 3,500 more calories. If you reduce your daily calories by just 500 each day (the max you should eliminate from your daily intake), you can lose 1 pound in one week.

To figure out how many calories you need to consume each day, check out the following sections.

Calculating the calories you burn just being alive

Your *basal metabolic rate* (BMR) is the basic number of calories you need every day to keep your body up and running and maintain your breathing, heartbeat, and body temperature. Everyone's BMR is different.

About 60 percent to 70 percent of your body's energy goes into pure maintenance. The other 30 percent to 40 percent is used for your daily activities. The more you do physically each day, the more calories you need.

A common BMR calculator is the Harris-Benedict formula:

- ✓ **Adult male:** 66 + (6.3 × body weight in pounds) + (12.9 × height in inches) – (6.8 × age in years)

- ✓ **Adult female:** 655 + (4.3 × weight in pounds) + (4.7 × height in inches) – (4.7 × age in years)

You can find a BMR calculator online at www.bmi-calculator. net/bmr-calculator.

Factoring in your activity level

Now you need to calculate how many calories you expend per day with physical activity. This formula is a bit more complicated. It uses an *activity multiplier* (a number that adjusts the calculation for activity levels) and your BMR (see the preceding section). Be honest about your activity level when figuring out how much you can eat each day.

You expend the following calories, depending on your lifestyle:

- ✓ Sedentary (little or no exercise, desk job) = BMR × 1.2

- ✓ Lightly active (light exercise one to three days a week) = BMR × 1.375

- ✓ Moderately active (moderate exercise three to five days a week) = BMR × 1.55

- ✓ Very active (hard exercise six to seven days per week) = BMR × 1.725

- ✓ Extremely active (hard daily exercise and a physical job) = BMR × 1.9

The number you get when you multiply your BMR times the number corresponding to your activity level tells you your total daily energy expenditure. For example, if your BMR is 1,339 calories and you're moderately active, your total daily energy expenditure is 1,339 × 1.55 = 2,075 calories per day.

Overcoming the urge to overeat

Overeating is a problem for many people trying to lose or maintain their weight. Although most excess body fat is caused more often by decreased physical activity than anything else, the truth is, eating too much, too often, is all too easy.

Here are some tips to prevent overeating:

- **Have a few sips of orange juice before you eat.** Several ounces of juice will raise your blood sugar and take the edge off your hunger pains.

- **Eat with company.** When you're eating alone and have no one to talk to, you're liable to overeat. Having the support of family and friends in reaching your goals can help you achieve them.

- **Start with smaller portions.** The first couple of times you put less food on your plate, your body may demand more, but stick with the program — your body will get used to smaller portions. If you're the type who just can't say no to a second helping of a tasty main course, help yourself to a second helping of salad or vegetables instead.

- **Eat slower.** When you wolf down your food in three minutes, you may want to extend the eating experience by scavenging for second helpings. Try setting down your fork in between bites to eat slower.

- **Eat some fruit between meals.** If you eat an orange or apple between lunch and dinner, the fiber helps keep you full, and you may be less hungry when you sit down to the dinner table.

- **Limit yourself to a couple desserts a week.** You can't have two or three desserts a day and expect to keep your weight down. But if you let yourself have one or two a week, you won't feel deprived. If you feel the need to have something sweet every day, choose small treats like bite-size candy bars or prepackaged portion-controlled dessert servings.

- **Drink plenty of water.** You're not going to be as hungry if you're drinking eight to ten glasses of water a day.

> ✔ **Use a fork and knife.** Even when you're eating pizza, use a fork and knife. Using utensils slows you down and enables you to take smaller bites. Taking smaller bites and chewing more enables you to savor your food longer; savoring your food longer means you may eat less.

Following the Ten Commandments of Nutrition

Eating well may be challenging, but it can be done, says Pamela Smith, nationally known nutritionist, author (*The Diet Trap* and *Eat Well, Live Well*), and culinary consultant from Orlando. And it's not as complicated as you think. Pam's "Ten Commandments of Great Nutrition" emphasize what you *should* eat, rather than what to avoid. Heed these commandments, and you won't wander 40 years in the fitness wilderness before reaching the promised land.

Thou shalt never skip breakfast

Your body awakens in a slowed-down state. When you don't eat breakfast, your body turns to its own muscle mass (not fat!) for energy. Your metabolism slows down even more, as your body conserves energy for a potentially long, starved state. Your next meal is not even burned for energy but is stored as fat as your body is trying to keep you from starving to death. You need to give your body a chance to boost its energy and raise its metabolism by feeding it some breakfast daily.

Thou shalt eat every three to four hours

Letting many hours pass between meals causes the body to slow down metabolically. When you allow too much time to pass between lunch and dinner, your dinner (healthy or not) is perceived as an overload; the nutrients are not being used optimally, and your lowered blood-sugar level leaves you sleepy and craving sweets. When you eat frequent, small meals, your body has a chance to metabolize those calories efficiently — burning those calories for energy instead of storing them as fat.

Several small meals a day deposit less fat than one or two large meals. You must keep your body fed with food at the right time to metabolize calories efficiently.

Thou shalt always eat a carb with a protein

Every meal (and snack) should include both carbohydrates and proteins. Carbohydrates — fruits, fruit juices, and non-starchy vegetables — provide 100 percent pure energy and fuel for your body. Proteins — meats and dairy products — are essential for your skin, bones, ligaments, and cell growth among other complex functions. When no carbohydrates are available, the body burns proteins. Eat a carbohydrate (like wild rice and a salad) with a protein (like a baked, skinless chicken breast) to protect the protein from being wasted as a less efficient fuel source.

Thou shalt double thy fiber

Increasing your fiber intake may be accomplished by eating wholesome foods prepared in a wholesome way:

- ✔ **Eat whole grain breads and cereals instead of white, refined types.** Look for "100 percent whole wheat" on the label with the word *whole* as the first ingredient on the list.

- ✔ **Eat fresh vegetables and fruits with well-washed skins.** Peel vegetables and fruits that have been waxed.

- ✔ **Choose raw or lightly cooked vegetables in a nonprocessed form.** As vegetables are ground, mashed, pureed, or juiced, the fiber effectiveness decreases.

- ✔ **Add a variety of legumes (such as peas or beans) to your diet.**

- ✔ **Add unprocessed oat or wheat bran to your foods.** Try eating bran as a hot cereal or by sprinkling it uncooked on your cold cereal.

Thou shalt trim the fat

Fat is a nutrient that the body needs in very limited amounts for lubrication and for transporting fat-soluble vitamins (A, D, E, and K). When eaten in excess, fat:

- ✔ Increases your cholesterol level and, in turn, your risk of heart disease and stroke

- ✔ Increases your risk of developing cancer, particularly of the colon

- ✔ Increases your risk of gall bladder disease

- ✔ Elevates your blood pressure, regardless of your weight

- ✔ Makes you fat

You need to eat carbohydrates and proteins at each meal, but you don't need fats in the quantities the average person consumes. Research shows that fats from foods are stored as fat on the body more readily than carbohydrates or proteins are. Fewer fats in your diet mean less fat on your body and less cholesterol in your blood.

Thou shalt believe thy mother was right: Eat thy vegetables

Vegetables and fruits are carbohydrates that provide a storehouse of vitamins, minerals, and other substances to protect against disease. Fruits and veggies are also valuable no-fat, no-cholesterol sources of fiber and fluid.

Generally the more vivid the fruit or vegetable's color, the more essential nutrients it holds. That deep orange or red coloring in carrots, sweet potatoes, cantaloupes, apricots, peaches, and strawberries signals their vitamin A content. Dark green leafy vegetables such as greens, spinach, romaine lettuce, Brussels sprouts, and broccoli are loaded with vitamin A as well as folic acid (a B vitamin that is essential for cell growth and reproduction). Vitamin C is found in more than just citrus fruits; it is also power-packed into strawberries, cantaloupes, tomatoes, green peppers, and broccoli. When fruits and veggies are loaded with color, they're loaded with nutrition!

Thou shalt get thy vitamins and minerals from foods, not pills

Can good nutrition be put into a capsule? No! Do you need to take vitamin-mineral supplements? It depends on your lifestyle choices.

Do you skip breakfast? Lunch too, sometimes? Do you eat on the run a lot? Eat out frequently? Drink alcohol? Have a high-stress career or home life? Drink coffee? If you answer yes to a few of these questions, your nutritional state may be at risk.

If you continue this lifestyle, you may benefit from supplemental vitamins and minerals. However, supplements may not be the answer to repairing your nutritional imbalance. You may remedy your situation by arranging your day to include balanced, wholesome meals and snacks, eaten at regular intervals.

Thou shalt drink at least eight glasses of water a day

Increasing your water intake to meet your body's needs may produce miraculous results. Water reduces fat deposits in the body, flushes out waste and toxins, helps maintain muscle tone, moisturizes skin, and even suppresses appetite.

How much water do you need? Eight to ten 8-ounce glasses each day. As you begin to meet this need by drinking more water, your natural thirst for it increases. As you figure out what water does for your body, your motivation for drinking it grows.

Try carrying a reusable water bottle with you during the day. You'll increase your water intake and reduce the impact on the environment by avoiding plastic throw-away bottles.

Thou shalt limit thy intake of sugar, salt, caffeine, and alcohol

Called by many names — honey, brown sugar, corn syrup, fructose — sugar is sugar. Sugar causes dental cavities, obesity, and mood swings; it wreaks havoc with diabetes and hypoglycemia. Cut back on your daily use of sugar and eat more fruit to satisfy your natural craving for a sweet taste.

As for salt, most people consume 5 to 25 times more salt than they need, leading to hypertension and kidney disease. Caffeine, a relatively mild stimulant, promotes irritability, anxiety, and mood disturbances.

And alcohol, one of the most common and addictive drugs of our time, is a factor in many killer diseases: *hypoglycemia* (abnormally low blood sugar), brain and heart damage, enlarged blood vessels in the skin, chronic gastritis, and *pancreatitis* (inflammation of the pancreas).

Thou shalt never go on a fad diet

The word *diet* can be a nasty four-letter word. Diet speaks defeat and depression and denotes temporary action. You may go on diets only to go off them. Diets don't work; they modify behavior only temporarily.

Break the diet mentality with a nutrition consciousness that works for life. You can feel better, have abundant energy from morning to night, and look healthier and more radiant. You need to take a second look at your eating habits. With your newfound knowledge about nutrition and the way your body works, you should never have to diet again!

Fit as a Fiddle: Exercising for Fitness and Lower Stress

What you eat is just one part of your physical health. Equally important is getting enough exercise. Exercise has numerous benefits:

- ✔ **It gives you energy.** A good workout releases enzymes that make you feel great.

- ✔ **It prevents muscle deterioration.** Beginning at around age 40, muscles shrink by 1 percent a year unless you embark on a consistent fitness program.

- ✔ **It makes your skin look better.** Exercise increases blood flow to the skin, giving you a healthy glow.

- ✔ **It helps prevent osteoporosis.** Exercise increases bone mass in both men and women as they age.

- ✔ **It helps prevent high blood pressure.** A healthy heart pumps stronger, which keeps arteries expanded.

- ✔ **It makes you fitter than young couch potatoes.** Studies show that middle-aged people have lower resting heart rates than inactive people in their 20s.

If your mind is already compiling a list of excuses, stop right there. We've got every excuse covered:

Excuse	*Counterpoint*
I'm too fat.	You'll weigh less if you start exercising regularly.
I'm too tired.	You won't be after you're finished exercising.
Walking hurts my knees.	Then ride a recumbent bike or swim.
I don't have the right shoes.	Invest in a pair of inexpensive sneakers.
I'm out of shape.	So? A thousand-mile journey begins with a single step.

In the following sections, we tell you how to create an exercise program you'll actually enjoy, and how to make it part of your life — a part you'll never want to give up!

Creating a safe and effective exercise program

After a doctor clears you to exercise, you should be able to compile a personalized exercise program. If you don't have the help of a personal trainer, set up a program based on your level of experience. This section guides the way.

Covering the bases: The components of a complete routine

A common misconception for people who are just starting a routine is to focus only on cardio. But in that case, your body burns the energy stored in your muscles first and burns fat only as a last resort. (We know — it's a frustrating arrangement!) So, a body transformation occurs most efficiently by *simultaneously* gaining muscle through strength training and losing fat through aerobics and diet. It's like a tricycle — all three wheels have to turn at the same time.

As you build your personalized program, be sure to include the following:

✔ **Aerobic training:** Activities like walking, swimming, and biking are all good for the heart and lungs.

✔ **Strength training:** This is the only activity that slows muscle and bone loss while it promotes weight loss.

If you're just beginning your strength training routine or you're a novice, we recommend strength training 20 to 30 minutes two to three days a week. If you're an old pro, you're most likely strength training 30 to 60 minutes four to five days a week, so keep it up! Don't forget to incorporate five to ten minutes of flexibility training to stretch your muscle groups before and after your strength training.

People over 60 who want to reduce their risk of falls and injury should start by strengthening their leg, arm, and core muscles with two to three days of weight training a week for three to four weeks before walking long distances or engaging in aerobic exercise.

✔ **Flexibility training:** To maintain good muscle health and reduce injury, we urge you to incorporate flexibility training through stretching, yoga, and Pilates. These activities not only feel good but also increase the range of motion of your joints.

People who have been sedentary for long periods (at least 6 to 12 months) may be at a higher risk for injury because muscle tone is weak, flexibility is limited, and balance is shaky. *Note:* Although most people consider walking the first step in becoming active, starting with strength training may be safer and more beneficial for people with limitations in their mobility (joint disease) or aerobic capacities (advanced lung disease).

If you haven't had much experience in the gym, start with some basic training. Many fitness centers offer circuit training, which consists of multiple machines with instructions and displays of the muscle groups that they target. You cycle through the machines, targeting all the muscle groups. You can increase the intensity as you go and concentrate on specific weak areas as you see fit. Aerobic activity can be worked into the schedule or you can alternate days between aerobic and strength training.

Factoring in your personality and lifestyle

When starting an exercise routine, you need to first evaluate your personality and lifestyle. If you create a routine that you don't enjoy, can't afford, or can't squeeze in, chances are good that you won't stick with it.

Ask yourself the following questions:

- **What motivates me?** Motivation (or the lack of it) has the power to start and stop a routine as fast as you can spit the word out. Paying for a membership gets some people to commit to the gym because they want to get their money's worth. Make a bet or a deal with a colleague, friend, or partner that involves exercise or weight-loss goals. You can get motivated, but sometimes you have to be creative.

- **Can I stick to my guns all on my own, or do I need the support of a group class, support group, planned weight-loss program, workout partner, or personal trainer?** Some people wake up one morning, make a decision to stop living life in an overweight or simply sedentary body, and change their habits instantly. Others have a bit more trouble following through. Maybe they need to socialize and engage with others who have the same goals to continue toward successfully achieving those goals.

- **What type of programs meet my health needs and interest me?** Carefully consider what keeps you coming back for more. For some people, various classes at the gym are helpful; for others, the commitment to an upcoming 5K or a mini-triathlon piques their interest. Some people train for the next Iron Man competition, and others with limiting health conditions may set a goal to maintain their current health.

✔ **What resources are available to me, and how much money am I willing to spend?** You can find an exercise program for any budget. Remember that allocating funds for your health is an investment that can reduce medical visits, medications, and time off work. It could be the best money you spend!

✔ **What time of day is best for me to work out?** There's really no perfect time of day that maximizes your workouts. The best time of the day is the time that's consistently available to you with the least interruptions.

From trial to style: Making a (good) habit of it

Whatever the reason for *starting* an exercise routine, you need to have even better reasons for *keeping* the fire burning. Too often, the smallest hurdle (a broken fingernail, a mild headache, or a friend saying, "Aw, do you have to work out today?") can put out that fire.

In general, you need to follow a routine for 21 days in order for it to become habit. And to achieve a healthy body weight and maintain it, you must truly believe that there are no shortcuts!

To help avoid this pitfall, keep these suggestions in mind:

✔ **Make exercise a priority.** Just like sleeping, eating, working, and spending time with your family — set a time in your schedule for exercise and stick to it.

✔ **Practice saying "no."** You can do this in a kind but firm way. When friends and family try to interfere with your workout plans, say no.

Your routine also affects the people closest to you; it takes them time to adjust as well. If you're consistent, you can ease resentment on both ends.

✔ **Implement a system of checks and balances.** Every decision you make requires some sacrifice to keep things in balance. (No one can have it all, do it all, or eat it all and reach their goals!) Balance is the key to life, and weight loss is no different. Trying to lose weight requires sacrifices every day — but those sacrifices are balanced by the rewards. You have to get yourself ready by recognizing the difficult situations that make it hard to make those sacrifices. For example, don't have candy in the house if you love candy. Out of sight, (hopefully!) out of mind.

Sacrifice is important, but torture is unnecessary. Make sure that you have checks in place to increase your chances of success. If you like coffee in the morning, have the coffee, but also drink more water. If you like to have a beer in the evening, switch to a light beer. If you want to have dessert on occasion, work out three days a week to balance out those calories.

Getting a Good Night's Sleep

As you age, you may become more prone to wakeful nights both because of natural age-related sleep cycle changes and other problematic causes. Until recently, research on sleep problems focused on the elderly. However, new research indicates that sleep disruptions start in middle age — the time of life when people are most productive. Hormonal changes combined with work- and family-related stressors are a recipe for sleepless nights.

Fortunately, armed with information, you can take steps to improve your quality of sleep, so that you're rested and ready to take on your day. We show you how in the following sections.

Recognizing how sleep changes as you age

As you get older, the following issues may contribute to poor sleep patterns:

- **Sleep hygiene:** Sleep hygiene is the practice of following simple guidelines to ensure restful, effective sleep. Irregular sleep/wake times, caffeine, alcohol, and daytime napping are all common examples of poor sleep hygiene. (For more on proper sleep hygiene, see the next section.)

✔ **Changes in the circadian rhythm:** *Circadian rhythms* are the powerful rhythms of the body that influence many different systems — sleep being one of them. People tend to sleep more lightly and for shorter time spans as they get older, although they generally need about the same amount of sleep as they needed in early adulthood.

✔ **Hormone changes:** Changes in a woman's body before and during menopause can cause severe disruptions to sleep, such as hot flashes, heart palpitations, and anxiety. In addition, decreases in both growth hormone and melatonin, two important hormones for sleep regulation, are among the bigger causes of sleep problems.

✔ **Pain:** Pain is a common reason for poor sleep in older people. From arthritis to heartburn, pain or discomfort is a common complaint as you age. Even minor aches and pains rob older people of sleep.

✔ **Bladder control problems:** Frequency or loss of control of urination may cause awakenings in both men and women and seem to increase with age.

✔ **Sleep disorders:** Conditions such as sleep apnea, restless leg syndrome, and insomnia are all commonly experienced as you age.

✔ **Prescription medications:** Some medications can interfere with sleep. Some antidepressants, nicotine, and beta blockers can affect the stages of sleep and how rested you feel.

Setting yourself up for sleep

Some of the most common causes of sleeping problems are completely preventable and fall under one category: sleep hygiene. Sleep hygiene isn't associated with cleanliness — it focuses on the everyday habits that induce good sleep.

Here are some bedtime tips for getting a good night's sleep:

✔ **Reserve the bed as a sacred place for sleeping (or sex).** Don't watch TV or read when you're in bed. The bed is a place for sleep; don't go there until you're ready for that commitment.

✔ **Go to bed and get up at the same time every day.** The easiest way to reset your rhythm when it's been thrown out of whack by travel, late nights, or illness is to get back to your targeted sleep/wake cycle and stick to it. The body functions well on a fixed schedule.

✔ **Steer clear of caffeine at least six hours prior to bed.** Some people are actually affected by caffeine longer than this timeframe, but six hours is a good general rule.

✔ **Exercise regularly but at a reasonable time.** Exercising regularly (at least 30 minutes a day; preferably in the morning) helps you sleep better at night. Remember to stay away from heavy exercise two to three hours before bed — the release of *endorphins,* which are natural stimulants, energizes and wakes up your body, and it can take a few hours to wind back down.

✔ **Eat your last meal or snack at least three hours before going to bed.** Avoid eating a large or high-sugar meal before bed. This intake can cause heartburn and other gastrointestinal upsets that interrupt sleep.

✔ **Avoid drinking alcohol four hours before bed.** Many people drink alcohol because they feel that it makes them sleep better. Yes, alcohol can make some people fall asleep, but the problem is that it often keeps you in the lighter stages of sleep.

✔ **Try not to nap during the day.** If you don't sleep well during the night, logically, you shouldn't sleep during the day so that you can establish a pattern. You may have to work hard at skipping that afternoon snooze to get into a good sleep pattern, but you can do it.

✔ **Consult your doctor about sleeping medications.** Don't take any sleeping medication — even over-the-counter ones — without consulting your doctor. You don't want to *treat* sleeping problems if you can *solve* them. Getting in sync may take a few days, but you'll feel better in the long run.

With a good night's sleep, you'll be ready to tackle your day!

Chapter 2

Mental Well-Being: Keeping Your Wits about You

In This Chapter

▶ Defying the cliché of the cranky old man or woman

▶ Reducing the stress in your life

▶ Exercising your brain

A positive attitude, along with a sense of general well-being, significantly enhances the quality of life for adults, as does improving your mind and memory through mentally stimulating exercises. This chapter helps you discover ways to foster happiness, decrease stress in your life, have a more positive outlook, and keep your mind razor-sharp.

Growing Happier

Remember the people you thought were "old" when you were growing up? Some of them were sharp as a tack, had a great sense of humor, and seemed just plain happy. Others were cranky and made you count the minutes until you could go out and play. You don't have to get cranky as you age. But happiness doesn't just happen — you have to work at it — and it's never too late or too early to start. In this section, we show you how.

The four basic ingredients of happiness

The foundation for true happiness consists of four basic ingredients:

✔ **Safety:** Not everyone lives in a safe world. There are unsafe neighborhoods, where crime is rampant and all the windows have bars. There are unsafe relationships, where a person's odds of being harmed — physically and/or emotionally — are exceedingly high. And, not everyone has a safety net when it comes to financial problems. Feeling unsafe carries with it fear, uncertainty, and bodily tension — hardly a context in which you can expect to be happy.

✔ **Satiation:** In simple terms, satiation means being full. A happy person is someone who, *at least at this moment,* is full. She has had enough of something (or things) she values.

You may be asking yourself, "But who decides when you have enough of something?" *You* do. It's just that simple. You, and only you, are the arbiter of how much is enough. If nothing is ever enough for you, your search for happiness is one without end!

No one has everything he wants. You may have enough money, but not enough friends. You may have plenty of friends, but not enough money. You can be happy even if your life isn't 100 percent "full," but you can't be happy if your life is empty.

✔ **Perspective:** Finding happiness requires that you take a step back from life and reflect on the bigger picture of what your life is all about. That's called *perspective* — and, in today's hectic world, not many of us have it! We're far too busy climbing or cutting down the trees in front of us to have any sense of the forest as a whole. What we really need is an aerial view of our own lives. Happiness, after all, is not about what you're doing at the moment — it's about the impact of what you're doing on your life, positive or negative. If the impact is positive, happiness follows. If it's negative, unhappiness follows.

✔ **Quietude:** Happiness cannot find you amidst a lot of noise — it finds you when you're in a quiet place or circumstance. You need a place where you can get in touch with the other three basic elements of achieving happiness, someplace where you can appreciate how safe you feel, where you can see how satiated you are, and where it's not so difficult to achieve some perspective. You have to get off the proverbial treadmill of daily life, stop running with the bulls (the ones that wear suits and ties, not the four-legged kind!), and rest.

What you're looking for is a place where you can hear yourself think, free of distractions or responsibilities. Ideally, you want to be able to spend at least 20 minutes a day in quietude. It doesn't have to be in the same place every day, though — one day you may find your quietude in your garden, the next day it may be at the beach. The important thing isn't where you find the quietude, it's that you find it in the first place, because, without it, you'll have trouble being happy.

How close are you?

If you want to know how close you are to happiness, answer the following questions — and be honest. Circle one answer per question.

1. **Generally speaking, how safe and secure do you feel in your everyday life?**

   Not at all: 1   A little: 2

   Fairly safe: 3   Very safe: 4

2. **All things considered, do you feel you have enough of what you need to be happy?**

   Not at all: 1   Possibly: 2

   Probably: 3   Absolutely: 4

3. **Do you have moments when you look at the totality of your life rather than just the events of the moment?**

   Not at all: 1   Occasionally: 2

   Regularly: 3   Quite often: 4

4. **How often do you find yourself in a quiet place or circumstance where you can have a moment of true self-reflection?**

   Never: 1   Seldom: 2

   Occasionally: 3   Very often: 4

5. **How satisfied are you with specific things in your life — finances, relationships, career?**

   Not at all: 1   Somewhat: 2

   Moderately: 3   Very much: 4

6. **How pleased are you with your general life situation?**

   Not at all: 1   A little: 2

   Moderately: 3   Very much: 4

7. **How grateful are you for the way your life is turning out?**

   Not at all: 1   Somewhat: 2

   Moderately: 3   Very much: 4

8. **How often do you have a sense of peace of mind?**

   Never: 1   Rarely: 2

   Occasionally: 3   Much of the time: 4

9. **How would you rate your overall state of mental and physical well-being?**

   Poor: 1   Average: 2

   Above average: 3   Excellent: 4

10. **How often do you find yourself experiencing a feeling of contentment?**

    Never: 1   Rarely: 2

    Occasionally: 3   Very often: 4

Add up the scores. If your total score is below 20, you're a long way from being a happy camper. If your score is 35 or above, you're either already happy or you're right on the verge. And if you're in between 20 and 35, you're neither happy nor miserable.

Take a minute and more closely examine your individual answers to the ten questions. Focus on those you had a low score on — either a 1 or 2. These are the missing ingredients from your recipe for happiness, and they're the ones that need your attention. By focusing on these missing ingredients, you move closer to your objective of being a happier person.

Decreasing Stress

Discovering how to manage and reduce your stress load may improve the quality of your life, and give you a better chance to live a long and healthier one. Lots of tools, tips, and techniques can help you reduce stress and figure out how to relax. Recognizing stress is the first and hardest thing for many people to do. Finding and focusing on sources of stress is helpful, because you're concentrating on what you can do to change rather than letting stress continue to grow until it's out of control.

With a little practice and creativity, you can reduce your stress levels and soon look forward to the newfound pleasure of relaxing your mind and body with the help of one of these stress busters.

Accentuating the positive

Researchers say that the people with more positive attitudes may deal with stress better and have a stronger will to live. People who feel good about themselves as they get older live about seven and a half years longer than the bitter, negative types. (For more proof, see the nearby sidebar, "The importance of a positive attitude.")

How can you keep a positive attitude? Two things that help are

✔ Accepting that you can't control some events in your life

✔ Being assertive and positive instead of aggressive in stressful situations

Part of staying positive is being able to see humor in situations, including those that may normally stress you out. Laughter really is the best medicine when it comes to reducing your stress. Laughing reduces the production of *cortisol* (which accelerates aging) and increases the level of health-enhancing hormones like endorphins and neurotransmitters. Laughter also increases the number of antibody-producing cells and enhances the effectiveness of T cells. What that boils down to is a stronger immune system and fewer physical effects from stress.

Putting self-relaxation techniques to work

Saying "Just relax" when your stress levels are building is easy, but actually doing it is much easier if you've developed some relaxation techniques. We offer a variety of methods in the following sections.

The importance of a positive attitude

Growing older brings major life changes, and staying positive and happy isn't always easy during the years when you may lose people near and dear to you, have unexpected health issues, need to move out of the family home for financial or health reasons, have children move away, or retire from a job that meant the world to you.

Yet, contrary to popular opinion, aging and a negative attitude don't go hand in hand. One large study reported in the *Journal of Personality and Social Psychology* that as people age, they become happier rather than sadder and are able to regulate emotions more effectively than younger adults. Even if you're not Mary Sunshine by nature, you can learn to develop a positive overall outlook.

Why bother? Although being optimistic isn't a surefire ticket to living into your hundreds, several studies have shown that pessimism can increase your risk of dying at a younger age. Consider the following studies:

✔ A study done in the Netherlands involving nearly 1,000 participants ages 65 to 85 showed that people who described themselves as being highly optimistic had a risk of dying that was 55 percent lower than the risk of pessimists during the ten-year study period. The risks of dying from heart disease were 23 percent lower for optimists during the same period.

✔ The Ohio Longitudinal Study of Aging and Retirement began in the 1970s with more than 1,100 people and concluded more than 20 years later with more than 600 people age 50 and older. The study showed that people with a healthy attitude toward aging lived more than seven years longer than those with a negative attitude.

✔ The Mayo Clinic reported that when psychological tests given to more than 800 people were reviewed, pessimistic people were 19 percent more likely to have died in any given year than optimists.

Like everything else, you can carry optimism too far, which can have grave consequences. Optimism can lead to a carefree attitude that results in unfortunate, but often avoidable problems resulting from taking risks when taking precautions would be the proper action. Excessive optimism can also lead to an overly trusting attitude, and some overly trusting seniors have been conned out of large sums of money by individuals or organizations. Again, balance is the key, and you have to have the right amount of positive thinking and common sense when it comes to your health, money, and other important life issues.

The bottom line? Being optimistic can help you live longer — but don't leave common sense at the door. In some situations, skepticism or a touch of pessimism may be the right choice.

Deep, slow breathing

Deep, slow breathing — the kind that reaches all the way into your gut, moving your abdomen out and in — is one of the easiest and most cleansing stress relievers with a variety of body-benefits. Deep breathing helps oxygenate your blood, which "wakes up" your brain, relaxes your muscles, and quiets your mind. You focus on relaxing your body and releasing air on each breath. Deep breathing is easy to practice because you can breathe anywhere, and it works quickly to relieve your stress.

Meditation

Meditation builds on the technique of deep breathing and goes one step further. After you master the technique of slow, deep, cleansing breaths to calm your body and restore and calm your breathing to a normal, relaxed state, you can begin to meditate. In some forms of meditation, your brain enters a state that's similar to sleep, but it carries some added benefits that you can't achieve as well in any other state, including the release of certain hormones that promote health. In other meditation techniques, the focus is on recognizing and accepting your feelings in the moment without trying to change them and without dwelling on them.

During meditation, you clear your mind of any focus or distraction. This enables you to detach from stressors and restores your body to a state of calm, essentially giving your body time to repair itself. Breathing returns to normal, so you use oxygen more efficiently. Your heart rate slows down, your blood pressure comes down, and anxiety levels decrease.

A tremendous benefit of meditation for anti-aging is that your adrenal glands produce less cortisol, adrenaline, and noradrenaline, which have been associated with negative effects on aging. By relaxing the body in this manner, you prevent damage from the physical effects of stress. Your body also makes additional positive hormones and your immune function improves.

Check out *Meditation For Dummies,* 2nd Edition, by Stephan Bodian (Wiley), for more information, including a CD with dozens of guided meditation exercises.

Guided imagery and visualization

Guided imagery and visualization techniques involve envisioning a relaxing scene or picturing yourself achieving goals or increasing your performance in some specific way. People who practice guided imagery go into a deeply relaxed state that provides significant stress-reduction benefits, including physically relaxing the body quickly and efficiently.

Progressive muscle relaxation

By tensing and relaxing all the muscle groups in your body you can relieve tension and feel much more relaxed in minutes, with no special training or equipment. Follow these steps:

1. **Start by tensing all the muscles in your face, holding a tight grimace for 10 seconds.**

2. **Completely relax the muscles from Step 1 for 10 seconds.**

3. **Repeat steps 1 and 2 with your neck, followed by your shoulders, and so on, all the way down to your toes.**

   You can do this exercise anywhere, and as you practice, you'll notice that you can relax more quickly and easily, reducing tension as quickly as it starts.

Using yoga

Yoga is an ancient path to spiritual growth. Today, *yoga* is a broad term for a series of personal stretches and exercises that bring together your physical, mental, and spiritual aspects of life. Yoga teaches you a series of stationary and moving poses called *asanas* and a form of breathing known as *pranayama*, as well as concentration techniques to help you get in tune with your body, your mind, and your emotions in the present moment. You can find many different schools of yoga, but they all have the goal of attaining a state of wholeness and completeness.

Yoga is designed to balance the different systems of your body. By taking your mind off the causes of stress, and having you gently stretch your body in ways that massage your internal organs, yoga helps you create an inner peace.

People of all ages can benefit from regular yoga practices, and with the various schools and the ability to change the poses, yoga can be adjusted to fit physical limitations and other complications.

For more information on yoga, check out *Yoga For Dummies,* by Georg Feuerstein, PhD, and Larry Payne, PhD (Wiley).

Working out in the bedroom

People often joke that the most uptight and stressed-out people may lighten up a bit if they just had sex. But there's truth there — the benefits of sex in stress reduction are plentiful. These benefits include deep breathing, lowering blood pressure, decreasing anxiety, getting a physical workout, and feeling a pleasurable sense of touch.

Most people feel the least like having sex when they're stressed out, but it's worth giving it some extra effort. Sexual activity releases endorphins and other feel-good hormones that put a smile on your face in no time.

Music

Music can be a powerful tool to aid relaxation and relieve stress. Music therapy has shown numerous health benefits for people with conditions ranging from stress to cancer. Music has been found to have an impact on hormones and neurotransmitters in the brain and has direct anxiety-lowering actions. Listening to, performing, or writing music can lower your blood pressure, relax your body, and calm your mind. It's often used as part of stress-management programs or in conjunction with exercise and is used in a variety of health-care settings with good results for dealing with illness and stress. Music therapy is an emerging field, one whose benefits are just now starting to be realized.

Exercising away your stress

Exercise is one of your body's best natural cures for stress. It leads to the release of endorphins, which has a healing effect on the body and mind and protects against some of the harmful effects of stress. Researchers have found that those who exercise have fewer stress-related health problems, which provides a positive impact on healthy aging.

Exercise can be as simple as a walk around your neighborhood every evening or as extensive as working out with a personal trainer. Find the type of exercise that works for you, your body, and your situation. For example, swimming is a great exercise if you suffer from arthritis and can't tolerate the joint-pounding strain of aerobic exercise. You may also find riding a stationary bike easier than running outdoors. Check out Chapter 1 for more exercise options.

Bringing out the kid in you

Life should be fun, and participating in activities you enjoy is a great way to relax and decrease stress. Having hobbies and outside interests keeps you connected and engaged with the world outside yourself.

Board games, puzzles, online games, crossword puzzles, and other fun activities can bring added joy and happiness to life, and they can be a great way to relieve stress. When you get really engrossed in an activity you enjoy, such as putting a puzzle together, you can experience a state of being known as *flow,* in which your brain is in a near-meditative state. This state benefits your body, mind, and soul.

Your stress level and your happiness benefit from at least one activity that you do regularly just for fun. Hobbies and games provide a fun way to sharpen skills, express your creativity, or just blow off steam.

Staying Sharp

Your mind may not be a muscle, but similar to your body, if you don't use it, you'll lose it. Especially as you age, using your mind is essential to staying sharp. In this section, we offer a couple techniques for exercising your mind. For even more memory-boosting tips, check out *Improving Your Memory For Dummies,* by John B. Arden, PhD (Wiley).

Building brain power with reasoning

Reasoning is an important — and practical — function of the brain. You can practice reasoning by asking the question "Why?" Children are great at this process and begin at about age 3. Every question is "Why?" Why does the dog have spots? Why are leaves green? Why are pillows soft? Children learn and discover the world this way, and you can stimulate your reasoning skills by doing the same.

Eating for a strong mind

What you eat and drink directly affects the chemistry of your brain and, thus, the keenness of your mind. For best results, adopt these habits:

✔ **Eat three balanced meals per day.** Each meal should consist of three parts: fruit or vegetable, complex carbohydrate (like whole-wheat bread), protein.

✔ **Stay hydrated.** Drink water and juices. Moderate your caffeine intake. Minimize sodas and sugar drinks.

✔ **Consider incorporating supplements as needed.** You may want to try vitamins, such as C, E, and the Bs; minerals, such as calcium, magnesium, and zinc; herbs, such as ginkgo (unless you're taking blood-thinning medications).

Just thinking about the possible answers to these questions forces your brain to use logic and intuition. Be just as curious about the world around you as a child, no matter how silly or reasonable your questions are.

Try this simple exercise:

1. **Pick an object, action, or topic to think about, and lie back and contemplate it for 30 minutes to an hour, working through all possible answers.**

2. **When you're tired of thinking, let it go and move on.**

   Some questions don't have answers, but they're still good to think about because of the strengthening effect they have on your mind and your ability to communicate reason.

Be careful not to let your thoughts drift toward a resentment or bad feelings you may be carrying when you're doing this exercise. Problem solving is great mental work, but the goal is to grow your mind, not wear it down.

Working crossword puzzles

Working crosswords can do for your mental health what walking does for your cardiovascular health. Plus, they're just plain fun!

Puzzle 1: Turn-Ons (Easy)

Across

1. Bat the breeze
5. Steakhouse order, perhaps
10. "Here comes trouble!"
14. "If I Were a ___ Man"
15. DNA structure
16. Space-race goal
17. ___ snuff (adequate)
18. "___ we all!"
19. Pierce player on *M*A*S*H*
20. Early yarn machine
23. Fiji's neighbor
24. Wee colonist
25. Talk, talk, talk
28. Start of a cheer
32. Greg's sitcom wife
34. Half-wit
38. Cafe au ___
39. He goes in circles
42. Tennis star Mandlikova
43. Porridge-type foods
44. With fervor
47. Bad to the bone
48. Herbal brew
49. Driver of a four-horse chariot, in myth
51. Jed Clampett portrayer Buddy
56. Certain halftime performers
61. The world, to Mr. Magoo

63. Pope John Paul II's first name
64. Strip the skin off
65. Vidal's Breckenridge
66. Play hard to get
67. "Beauty ___ the eye . . ."
68. What some willows do?
69. "Walk Away ___" (Four Tops)
70. Baby duster

Down

1. The mashed potatoes on shepherd's pie
2. *Fantasia* ballerina
3. Be a cast member of
4. Beachwear that leaves little to the imagination
5. Cambodian's neighbor
6. Swiss capital
7. Mr. Cassini
8. Old Japanese mercenary
9. Stretch outward
10. Arabian monarchy
11. Famed chalice
12. East of Eden
13. Stop ___ dime
21. Bellybutton
22. Nonacademic degree
26. Out of order
27. Financial shellacking
29. Roll call reply in French class

30. Italian wine
31. Aquarium microorganisms
33. Thomas ___ Edison
34. "___ a dream" (Martin Luther King)
35. Kind of golf
36. One of the Brady Bunch
37. 1999 Ron Howard film
39. "Huh?"
40. Beatles label
41. Make available to new tenants
45. Island necklace
46. *The New* ___ (humor magazine)

50. Bondservant
52. Suit
53. Dance or sauce
54. Correspondence created on keyboards
55. Former boy band
57. Fur stole
58. Ayatollah's land
59. Lymph, for one
60. Feeling of delight
61. Pricey wheels
62. Caustic substance

Puzzle 2: On Tap? (Tricky)

Across

1. Hinged implement
6. Industrial haze
10. Like Dorothy's slippers
14. Certain Nordic person
15. River to the Rhine
16. Big pot of stew
17. Draft
19. E pluribus ___
20. Judge Lance
21. Resort town near Santa Barbara
22. Joe-to-go packets?
24. What two fins equal
26. Go well together
27. Norse god of war
28. Post-arson markdown
32. Victrola successor
35. Push-button predecessor
37. Firmaments
38. "Oh, you wish!"
39. Bee "bite"
41. Significant times, historically
42. Office workers, collectively
44. Disaster ___
45. Proof goof
46. Unwanted overhang
48. Fond du ___, Wisconsin
50. Lean (on)
51. Seasoned vet
55. San Fernando Valley city
58. Ignored the limit
59. Peeples or Long
60. Ellery contemporary
61. Draft
64. Actress Cameron
65. Lady who rings doorbells
66. What a glass of warm pop has?
67. Treater's words
68. They have many teeth
69. Knight's mare

Down

1. Implicit
2. Stand up and speak
3. Synthetic textile
4. Cowpoke's sweetie
5. Charles Schulz character
6. 1978 co-Nobelist Anwar
7. Wailuku's isle
8. Food scrap
9. Yellowstone attraction
10. Draft
11. Elbow-to-wrist bone
12. Obscure
13. Oft-candied tubers
18. Norwegian bays
23. Plays for a sucker

25. Good thing for a cooling-off period?

26. Creator of a storybook Robin

28. Kind of tale

29. Well-ventilated

30. Clear a hurdle

31. Old gas station identification

32. Padlock mate

33. "That's all there ___ it!"

34. Royal order

36. Boot-shaped country

40. Ship's mess

43. Satellite transmission

47. Andean beasts

49. Enhancing accessories

51. Hangs out one's shingle

52. Bill's *Groundhog Day* costar

53. Sibling's daughter

54. Had the nerve

55. Go back to the drawing board

56. Green land?

57. It's grand in baseball

58. What a plow plows

62. Reproductive cells

63. Fall into decay

Puzzle 1: Turn-Ons

C	H	A	T		T	B	O	N	E		O	H	N	O
R	I	C	H		H	E	L	I	X		M	O	O	N
U	P	T	O		A	R	E	N	T		A	L	D	A
S	P	I	N	N	I	N	G	J	E	N	N	Y		
T	O	N	G	A			A	N	T		G	A	B	
		V	I	V	A		D	H	A	R	M	A		
	I	M	B	E	C	I	L	E		L	A	I	T	
W	H	I	R	L	I	N	G	D	E	R	V	I	S	H
H	A	N	A		O	A	T	M	E	A	L	S		
A	V	I	D	L	Y		E	V	I	L				
T	E	A		E	O	S			E	B	S	E	N	
		T	W	I	R	L	I	N	G	T	E	A	M	S
B	L	U	R		K	A	R	O	L		F	L	A	Y
M	Y	R	A		E	V	A	D	E		I	S	I	N
W	E	E	P		R	E	N	E	E		T	A	L	C

Puzzle 2: On Tap?

T	O	N	G	S		S	M	O	G		R	U	B	Y
A	R	Y	A	N		A	A	R	E		O	L	L	A
C	A	L	L	O	F	D	U	T	Y		U	N	U	M
I	T	O		O	J	A	I		S	U	G	A	R	S
T	E	N	S	P	O	T		M	E	S	H			
			T	Y	R		F	I	R	E	S	A	L	E
H	I	F	I		D	I	A	L		S	K	I	E	S
A	S	I	F		S	T	I	N	G		E	R	A	S
S	T	A	F	F		A	R	E	A		T	Y	P	O
P	O	T	B	E	L	L	Y		L	A	C			
			R	E	L	Y		O	L	D	H	A	N	D
R	E	S	E	D	A		S	P	E	D		N	I	A
E	R	L	E		M	O	N	E	Y	O	R	D	E	R
D	I	A	Z		A	V	O	N		N	O	I	C	E
O	N	M	E		S	A	W	S		S	T	E	E	D

Chapter 3

Financial Well-Being: Successfully Navigating the Waters

. . . .

In This Chapter

▶ Saving for retirement

▶ Drawing on retirement income

▶ Maximizing your estate

. . . .

*A*s you age, finances are a major concern — regardless of whether you've planned for it. The good news is, it's never too late to start planning for retirement! In this chapter, we answer your questions about saving for retirement, retirement income (including Social Security), and estate planning.

Discovering the Best Ways for You to Save for Retirement

You can use many options to save for retirement. However, these vehicles aren't created equal. In this section, we cover a variety of retirement savings vehicles, starting with the ones we recommend the most.

401 (k) and 403 (b) plans

If you have a 401(k) or 403(b) plan through your employer and your employer provides a matching contribution, fund this account up to the limits of the matching contribution. For example, say that your employer matches 50¢ on every dollar that you contribute to your 401(k), up to 6 percent of your annual salary. Your salary of $50,000 × 0.06 (amount matched) equals an annual contribution of $3,000; plus, you'll receive another $1,500 from your employer matching contribution, giving you a total of $4,500 per year.

By participating in your qualified retirement plan at work and receiving a matching contribution from your employer, you're receiving a guaranteed rate of return of no less than 50 percent per year.

Individual retirement accounts

There are two main types of individual retirement accounts (IRAs):

- ✔ **Traditional IRA:** You get a tax break when you contribute to a traditional IRA, but you pay taxes on the income when you withdraw it. If you expect to be in a lower tax bracket when you retire than you're in now, a traditional IRA may be right for you.

- ✔ **Roth IRA:** You receive no tax deduction by contributing to a Roth IRA account; however, all earnings accumulate on a tax-deferred basis, and all withdrawals taken out during retirement are tax-free. You never have to pay tax on the earnings in this account.

The Roth IRA is one of the most underappreciated and underused retirement vehicles available today. Everyone who qualifies to make a Roth IRA contribution and still needs to save for retirement should do so by utilizing a Roth.

Check with your financial advisor, go to www.irs.gov/
pub/irs-pdf/p590.pdf, or call 800-829-3676 and request
Publication 590 to get the latest rules on income and how
much you can contribute per year, as these numbers change
regularly.

When You Can Access Retirement Income

When you retire and no longer earn a paycheck, you'll need to
get income from somewhere. If you plan well, you'll have that
income available from these sources.

Social Security

The first source of income you'll have during retirement is
Social Security, the federal government's social insurance program that pays monthly benefit payments to retirees. Every
worker who earns enough credits (by working) is eligible for
Social Security benefits in retirement.

Many people mistakenly think that they'll start receiving
Social Security checks when they turn 65. In fact, for anyone
born after 1937, the age to receive full Social Security benefits
(called the *normal retirement age*) is at least a couple months
past their 65th birthday. If you were born in 1960 or later, you
won't be eligible for full Social Security benefits until your
67th birthday.

You *can* choose to receive reduced benefits at age 62 (even if
you were born in 1960 or later). If you retire at age 62, your benefits are reduced to 80 percent of the full benefit if 65 is your
normal retirement age, and 70 percent of the full benefit if 67
is your normal retirement age. Keep in mind that you'll always
receive the reduced benefits if you retire at age 62; they won't
increase when you reach your normal retirement age.

Table 3-1 shows the full retirement age for different birth
years after 1937.

Table 3-1 Social Security Full Retirement Age and Reduction in Benefits for Early Retirement

Year of Birth (If you were born on January 1, refer to the previous year)	Full Retirement Age	Total Reduction in Benefits If You Retire at 62
1937 or earlier	65 years	20%
1938	65 years, 2 months	20.83%
1939	65 years, 4 months	21.67%
1940	65 years, 6 months	22.50%
1941	65 years, 8 months	23.33%
1942	65 years, 10 months	24.17%
1943–1954	66 years	25%
1955	66 years, 2 months	25.83%
1956	66 years, 4 months	26.67%
1957	66 years, 6 months	27.50%
1958	66 years, 8 months	28.33%
1959	66 years, 10 months	29.17%
1960 and later	67 years	30%

Source: Social Security Administration (www.ssa.gov).

In sum, you can't expect to receive any retirement benefits from Social Security before age 62, and you can increase the amount you receive if you wait until 65, 66, or 67 (whatever your "normal retirement age" is), or even 70.

Some years ago, the Social Security Administration (SSA) began mailing annual statements to workers who are over 25 years old. These statements estimate how much money they'll receive monthly at age 62, at full retirement age, and at age 70, based on their income to date. If you threw yours away or can't find it, you can contact the SSA for a new one at www.ssa.gov/mystatement or by calling 800-772-1213.

Other sources

Now, what about your other sources of income during retirement? The following list highlights possible retirement resources above and beyond Social Security:

- ✔ **401(k):** As long as you're working for the employer that sponsors the plan, you generally can't take money out of a 401(k) before you're 59½. If your plan does permit you to withdraw money, you have to pay taxes and an extra early withdrawal penalty on the money you take out. If you leave your job at age 55 or older, you can withdraw the money without any penalty tax, but you still have to pay income tax. You can also roll it over into an IRA.

- ✔ **Other tax-favored retirement accounts:** Accounts similar to a 401(k), such as a 403(b) or IRA, have rules similar to those of 401(k)s. Generally, you can't count on having easy access to your money before age 59½, or possibly age 55. The rules are different for 457 "deferred-comp" plans. In some circumstances, you may be able to get at your retirement account money before age 55 without paying an early withdrawal penalty.

- ✔ **Traditional defined-benefit pension plan:** If your employer offers one of these plans, your human resources or benefits representative may be able to tell you what your expected payment will be if you qualify to receive benefits.

- ✔ **Life insurance:** Some people buy a type of life insurance policy that allows them to build up a cash account (a *cash value* policy) instead of buying term life insurance, which is worth nothing after you stop making payments. If you have a *cash value policy* (such as whole life or variable life), it should have a cash account that you can tap at retirement.

- ✔ **Regular taxable savings:** A taxable account is any kind of account (such as a bank account, mutual fund account, or stock brokerage account) that doesn't have special tax advantages.

- ✔ **Part-time work:** No matter when you retire, you may want to take a part-time job that will keep you active and give you extra income.

- ✔ **Inherited wealth:** You shouldn't count on any inheritance until you actually receive it. But if you do inherit a substantial amount of money, integrate at least part of it into your overall financial plan, to give yourself a higher retirement income.

If you plan to retire before age 65, don't forget to factor in the cost of medical insurance. The availability and cost of medical care is a major issue if you plan to retire before you and your spouse are eligible for Medicare, the government-sponsored medical program for those age 65 and older.

Estate Planning Basics

You can decide to leave what happens to your estate after you die totally up to chance (or, more accurately, the complicated set of state laws that will apply if you haven't done the estate planning that you need to do). But, chances are, the two fundamental goals of estate planning — protection and control — are top of mind.

In this section, we help you choose a will or trust (or both) for your estate. We also tell you what kinds of insurance you need to consider for your estate in order to protect your assets.

Writing a will or creating a trust for your estate

The revocable living trust is probably the most heavily marketed estate-planning tool in history. You create this trust during your lifetime and may amend or revoke it as you wish. The trust becomes irrevocable upon your death, and the trust's assets are distributed according to your instructions.

Marketing materials may leave you with the impression that everybody needs a living trust. By comparison, a will may seem ordinary. Don't be fooled. Your will is a failsafe for your estate plan. You may not need a trust, but you do need a will.

What a will can do for you

A *will* is the easiest tool to direct your assets to your beneficiaries. Your probate estate includes the property owned by you at the time of your death.

Your will designates the *personal representative* (executor) for your estate. If you wish, most states permit you to waive any bond that your personal representative is otherwise required to post under state law.

You can use your will to create a trust, often called a *testamentary trust,* to hold and distribute some or all of your assets. You can also provide that part of your estate, or the balance of your estate after your bequests, will go into an existing trust. A will that funds an existing trust is known as a *pour-over will.*

If you have minor children, you should designate a custodian for your children in your will. A court will review your designation and confirm that it is consistent with your children's needs, but courts usually defer to a parent's preference. You can designate the same person, or if you prefer a different person, to act as custodian of your children's assets.

Some of your assets, such as insurance and financial accounts with designated beneficiaries, or the assets you've transferred into your living trust, aren't included in your probate estate and, thus, aren't affected by your will.

What a trust can do for you

Many different types of trusts are available, each of which potentially provides a different set of benefits to your estate. Potential benefits of estate planning with trusts include avoiding probate, increased privacy, avoiding taxes, succession planning for your family business, and controlling the distribution of your estate.

Here are the trusts to consider:

- A **revocable living trust** is an excellent tool to plan for incapacity and the distribution of your assets, but it's a poor tool for avoiding estate taxes.

- **Charitable trusts** and **insurance trusts** may help you avoid estate taxes but aren't tools for distributing assets to your heirs.

- **Asset protection trusts** can help protect your financially troubled heirs from losing their inheritance to creditors.

The most popular trust is the *revocable living trust*. You transfer ownership of your assets into a trust that becomes active upon your death or legal incapacity. At that time, a trustee who you picked manages your estate consistent with instructions you included in your trust. After you die, trust assets are distributed to your heirs without going through probate.

Trusts give you great flexibility in planning bequests. For example, you can delay the age at which your children inherit assets, provide income and support for your heirs prior to distributing the bulk of your estate, or provide an inheritance in several installments.

Why you may benefit from a will and trust

If you don't have a will to back up your trust, anything that isn't included in your trust will go through probate. Those assets pass by the *laws of intestate succession,* meaning that the court determines who inherits your estate and what they inherit by state law.

Even if you carefully convey ownership of your property into a living trust, you'll have personal property when you die. You'll have clothes in your closet, cash in your wallet, and other items of personal property that must be conveyed to your heirs. You can use a will to do that, or you can use your will to direct your remaining property into your trust.

In many cases, significant assets are never transferred into a living trust. We've even encountered a very expensive, professionally prepared estate plan where *nothing* had been transferred into the trust. The trust was a thing of beauty, but the entire estate went through probate.

The choice is not between a will and a living trust. Your estate plan should include a will. You may benefit from also having a trust.

For much more information on wills and trusts, turn to *Wills & Trusts Kit For Dummies,* by Aaron Larson (Wiley).

Considering insurance

For your estate planning, as well as your day-to-day needs, consider the types of insurance discussed in the following sections.

Make a consolidated list of all insurance coverage you have from all the listed types, including the name(s) of insurance companies, contact information at the insurance company, policy numbers, and the location of the actual policy documents that are probably jumbled amidst all kinds of other important papers somewhere in your house!

For a far more comprehensive discussion about various types of insurance than we can provide in the limited space we have, check out *Insurance For Dummies,* 2nd Edition, by Jack Hungelmann (Wiley).

Life insurance

Life insurance works on a simple premise: If you die while you have a life insurance policy in effect, the insurance company pays money to your beneficiaries. Of course, the details are a bit more complicated, particularly around who receives the money and how much.

Here's why you need life insurance:

- ✔ **To replace your income if you die:** You may plan on earning income from your job or business for years to come. But suppose you die unexpectedly? Can your family get by on what you've saved so far plus your spouse's income? Or will your family be forced to sell the house and scale back dramatically to try to make ends meet because you're no longer around to provide for your family? One of the primary purposes of life insurance is to replace income that you would have otherwise earned if you were still alive.

- ✔ **To improve your estate's liquidity:** *Liquidity* is a financial term that basically means readily available cash or an asset that can be quickly turned into cash. Suppose that when you die you have a substantial estate worth $5 million, but almost all your estate is in your primary residence, your two vacation homes, and your investment in your business. You may have heard the old saying, "Rich people don't have any money," or the one that goes, "All his money is tied up in wealth." The point is, even if you're well off financially, your personal representative may not be able to distribute large sums of cash very easily, depending on the particular investment portfolio. So if your family needs money for living expenses or for some other substantial cash needs after you die, life insurance can be an important tool to provide cash without your family or other beneficiaries having to sell property that they otherwise wouldn't sell.

- ✔ **To pay off your debts:** Life insurance can provide money to pay off your estate's debts — mortgages on real property, business loans, and even sizable personal loans.

- ✔ **To provide money for estate taxes:** Instead of your family having to sell property to come up with money for estate taxes, life insurance proceeds can do the trick.

What if you don't have a spouse and children?

The common conventional wisdom about life insurance is that you need to provide money for your spouse and dependent children in the event of your death. But if you don't have to worry about paying for your children's college education after you're gone, or to provide money for your spouse to keep paying the mortgage on your house, then you probably don't need insurance. Therefore, the equation may be stated as "no spouse and kids = no life insurance needed."

Not so fast! Suppose that you're an avid supporter of a charitable cause, such as a small local animal shelter, and you regularly give hundreds of dollars each month to the charity and plan to do so for years to come. Perhaps, you're one of the shelter's primary benefactors. So what happens if you die suddenly, especially if you have a fairly modest estate without a lot of assets? Even if you leave your entire estate to the charity, you're only talking about a fraction of the total amount of money that would otherwise be available if you remain alive for many years and keep making your regular monthly contributions.

In this case, you may want a life insurance policy to make sure that even if you were to suddenly die, money would be available for the charity as if you were still alive and donating a portion of your salary every month.

Health insurance

Hopefully, you have some form of health insurance, either through your job or business or through some other source (such as an association to which you belong). If you don't have health insurance, you run a very high risk of watching much of your estate suddenly get whisked away to pay for medical bills.

Many people are accustomed to health insurance in the form of health maintenance organization (HMO) or preferred provider organization (PPO) coverage, where your primary interaction (and concern) is how much your deductible is for office visits and prescriptions. But at the most basic level, you must view health insurance as a means to help you pay for very high (and usually unexpected) health-related costs, such as extended treatment for cancer, care and rehabilitation after a heart attack or stroke, or any one of numerous other medical catastrophes that could befall you.

So from an estate-planning perspective, make sure that you clearly understand the details of your health-insurance policy beyond the deductible amounts printed on your insurance card. Pay particular attention to any maximum amounts associated with your policy, such as the maximum payment for a particular incident or any maximum lifetime benefits. Also, understand deductible amounts (if any) for hospitalization. If your insurance policy covers 80 percent of hospitalization costs (versus 100 percent) and you find yourself paying 20 percent of a very expensive prolonged stay for a serious accident or illness, your estate could get hit with a fairly heavy bill.

Selecting the most appropriate health insurance coverage isn't simply a matter of looking for a plan with the lowest possible premium payments or *first dollar coverage* (that is, all medical expenses are covered by the insurance, but you pay a much higher premium). You need to look at what's covered and what isn't — and how much the "what isn't" may cost you — and consider the impact on your estate plan if any worst-case scenarios come to pass and you need to lay out a lot of money.

Disability income insurance

Disability income insurance (often referred to as simply *disability insurance*) provides you with protection against a serious illness or injury that affects your ability to earn a living. Basically, if you get hurt or sick and can't work — but unlike with life insurance, you're still alive — disability insurance provides payments to cover living expenses and replace income.

You typically come across two different types of disability insurance, usually provided by or made available through your employer (though if you're self-employed, you can buy disability policies, just as you can buy health insurance or other forms of insurance). The two types are

- ✔ **Short-term disability,** which usually covers a period of three months (sometimes longer) and is often provided by using your current and sometimes future vacation balance

- ✔ **Long-term disability,** which as you may guess from the name, covers long periods of time — up to many years — by replacing a sizable portion of your income

You find all kinds of variations with long-term-disability insurance, so make sure you fully understand what your benefits are if you need to use the insurance. For example, some policies cover a fixed percentage of your salary — often around 60 percent to 67 percent — while other policies give you a choice as to how much of your salary is provided, ranging from 50 percent to 75 percent (with correspondingly higher or lower premium payments).

Other policies come into effect only if you're totally disabled, while still other more expensive policies may come into effect if you can't work in your chosen profession but still can perform some other type of paid work.

Some policies have a cost-of-living adjustment feature (that is, the payments go up each year according to increases in inflation rates or some other cost-of-living measure) — something to pay attention to if you're dealing with several decades of coverage because of disability.

Finally, most long-term disability policies provide coverage until the age of 65 (at which time government-provided health benefits can kick in), unless you want to buy coverage for a shorter period of time (for lower costs, of course).

If you can't work due to an illness or injury and you don't have long-term disability insurance, you can lose nearly everything. You may have to withdraw cash in your accounts and sell all your personal and real-estate property to make up for the lost income. From a medical perspective, you can at least receive rudimentary care through government-provided programs for those who can't pay, but at quite a price. Essentially, if you fail to protect against the loss of future income, you may lose everything you already have.

Long-term-care insurance

Long-term-care insurance is somewhat similar to long-term-disability insurance. Whereas long-term-disability insurance provides you a salary when you're unable to work, long-term care insurance covers the costs of long-term healthcare, such as nursing-home coverage.

You need to look at both long-term-disability insurance and long-term-care insurance in concert with one another, evaluating income replacement needs, what amount of healthcare costs you need to cover, and other financial and personal factors.

Think of long-term-care insurance as a cross between health insurance and long-term-disability insurance. Ask your insurance agent to help you figure out how much coverage you need to cover medical expenses, and how this coverage can be tied into your long-term-disability insurance. Also, ask if the insurance policies have any gaps in how they relate to one another. For example, you max out your health insurance, but a particular long-term-care policy doesn't kick in for one reason or another, essentially leaving you without coverage (and subjecting your estate to the lack of protection that you're trying to avoid in the first place through insurance).

Automobile insurance

For estate-planning purposes, you need to focus on the liability coverage provided by your automobile insurance policy.

Many people gloss over the confusing language in automobile policies about liability limits, wondering what the big deal is about "per person" and "per accident" amounts. Work with your insurance agent — or if you don't have an insurance agent, an insurance company representative with whom you speak over the phone when you set up or modify your policy — to thoroughly understand what the language in your policy (or the policy you're considering) means.

When working with your insurance agent, go through several accident scenarios involving one or more vehicles, one or more other people, and other factors to understand what your policy covers, and — even more important — what your policy doesn't cover. Then take a look at the impact on your estate plan, particularly how the policy can help protect what you have (in this case, from the result of a lawsuit or out-of-court settlement).

Homeowner's or renter's insurance

As with automobile insurance, you must consider the liability protection component with your homeowner's or renter's insurance policy if an accident happens on your property and someone sues you. Make sure that you clearly understand what's covered and what isn't.

As with most types of insurance, you're trying to prevent assets you currently have from being taken away. Ask your insurance agent to clearly explain any worst-case scenarios that may be expensive and may adversely impact your estate plan.

Umbrella liability insurance

Even though you probably have some degree of liability coverage through your automobile and homeowner's or renter's insurance policy, you may need additional liability insurance. Basically, the more your estate is worth, the more likely it is that someone will sue you in the event of an automobile accident or an injury on your property.

An *umbrella policy* provides additional coverage above and beyond your other liability coverage. Furthermore, the policy helps protect you against a financially devastating judgment in a lawsuit (or even a settlement to which you agree). As with the other types of insurance coverage we discuss in this chapter, stress to your insurance agent that you want to protect the property in your estate.

 Remember the question that we use several times in this chapter — "What is the worst-case scenario, and how will my estate plan be affected?" You must always ask your insurance agent this question about any type of insurance and the various policy options you consider. Make sure that you clearly understand the answer and that you balance all the insurance costs with what you have at stake. Again, a good insurance agent can help you protect what you can't afford to lose without trying to gouge you with very expensive coverage that essentially over-insures you.

When to review your estate plan

You should review your estate plan periodically to be sure that it's consistent with your needs and goals. In addition, review your estate plan upon:

✔ Marriage, separation, or divorce

✔ Birth or adoption of a child

✔ Death of a spouse or heir

✔ Moving to another state

✔ Significant changes in your health

✔ Significant changes in your financial condition

Chapter 4

Social Well-Being: Staying Connected

*B*arbra Streisand sang it best, "People who need people are the luckiest people in the world." According to a social survey, the importance of family relationships and good health are the two highest-rated variables when measuring happiness. Why? The ability to form deep, lasting bonds with other people through which you can share life experiences, learn, grow, trust, and support one another fulfills a fundamental human need. The absence of such relationships and bonds can lead to isolation and depression.

How do the relationships with the people in your life affect your attitude about getting older and how you spend your days? In this chapter, we look at how staying in touch with your nearest and dearest can positively contribute to both your mental and physical well-being. We also give you tips for staying connected, both online and off. With all the resources available today, you have no excuse for being isolated from the people you love, or not forming new friendships with people you share common interests with.

Connecting with Others

Your family and friends may be your most critical lifeline. Numerous studies have shown that having a strong social network results in a longer, healthier, and happier life. Although keeping in touch with friends and family far away or making new friends may be difficult, the long-term results are worth it.

Keeping in touch with friends and family

How can you stay in touch with family or friends who live scattered around the country? How can you remain close to those who live nearby without becoming a nuisance? Read on.

When you live nearby

When you live around the corner from family and friends, you may need to walk a fine line between being in touch and being in touch *too much*. Gauging the proper balance between closeness and too much togetherness isn't always easy, but, by using common sense, you can maintain close relationships without overstepping boundaries.

If you have close family and/or friends nearby, it may be beneficial for both of you to have definite times to get together instead of just dropping in and being dropped in on. Making "dates" to get together once a week, once a month, or once a day — whatever suits your particular lifestyle (and theirs) — gives both of you the freedom to plan your day and to know that you'll be seeing each other regularly.

When miles separate you

Staying connected to loved ones who are many miles away has never been easier. With cellphones that transmit pictures instantly, text messaging, e-mail, and webcams that connect your computer screen to theirs and allow you to see the person you're talking to, you need never be out of touch with the ones you love. (Visit www.skype.com to make free video phone calls.)

And if you need to see people in person to feel connected, airlines offer dozens of flights a day to wherever you want to go. Airfares vary considerably, so get familiar with Web sites like www.orbitz.com and www.expedia.com, which offer discounted flights, hotels, and car rentals.

Connecting to grandchildren

Being a grandparent can be really fun. Grandchildren bring all the joy of children with none (or at least less) of the hassles! Being a grandparent (and a good one at that) takes practice but brings rewards almost greater than any other relationship as you age. If you don't have any grandchildren, you can always volunteer at school functions or get involved with organizations such as Big Brothers Big Sisters to develop meaningful relationships. Some hospitals also have an "Adopted Grandparent" program for hospitalized children.

What makes a wonderful grandparent?

✔ **Love your grandchildren unconditionally.** This one comes naturally to most grandparents!

✔ **Respect their parents.** This is often a tough one; respecting their parents means following their rules for child rearing, supporting them in their decisions, and not sneaking forbidden goodies to your grandchild behind their parents' backs.

✔ **Know your boundaries.** Holding back on visiting or being involved with grandchildren's lives can be hard, but their parents' wishes must be paramount. Visit as often as you're invited — not as often as you want — and your relationship will be much happier.

Although all the modern methods of connection are wonderful, don't forget one of the old-fashioned — and certainly more permanent — ways of staying in touch — letter writing. Although it's becoming a forgotten art, letter writing not only is a way to stay in touch but also leaves a permanent legacy of your thoughts and day-to-day life behind.

For more great ways of staying in touch with people far and wide, check out "Keeping Your Social Network Going Strong with Technology," later in this chapter.

Making new friends

When you're younger, work relationships and parenting relationships lead naturally to friendships, but when you're older, meeting new people can be more difficult.

TIP

Finding new friends can be fun! Here are some tips:

- **Take classes.** Many towns have continuing education classes for adults of all ages. You can learn a new language or learn to paint — and make new friends in the process.

- **Join a gym or the local YMCA.** Not only will you reap the physical benefits of exercise, but you'll be surrounded by people who share your interest in fitness.

- **Volunteer for a cause or organization you support.** You'll find like-minded people who share your passion.

- **Join an organized sports league, such as bowling or softball.** You'll be doing an activity you enjoy, with people who enjoy it, too!

- **Join a book group.** Many bookstores — from the small independent ones to the big-name chains — sponsor book groups. Whether you're a fan of mysteries or histories, you'll find a group that meets your needs.

TIP

The key is to participate in an activity that you'll enjoy. Then, making new friends will be icing on the cake!

Keeping Your Social Network Going Strong with Technology

Years ago, phone calls and letters were the only ways to stay in touch with people. But now you have all kinds of options for keeping up with the people you care about, especially if you're connected to the Internet. In this section, we introduce you to three of the most popular social networking sites, Facebook, LinkedIn, and Twitter, and give you a taste of what each is like (as well as how they differ).

Facebook

Facebook (www.facebook.com) is one of the fastest growing phenomena of the 21st century. It provides a free and easy way to connect with those you know and love, as well as rediscover those you used to know. With more than 400 million people signed up, it's a great way to share, interact, and keep in touch with those important to you.

Here are some of the reasons you might want to use Facebook:

✔ **To keep in touch with your family:** These days, families are often spread far and wide across state or country lines. Facebook offers a place where families can meet and interact. Your kids can upload photos of the grand-kids for everyone to see; you can write notes about what you're up to and respond to what your kids and grand-kids are doing; and you can get a fuller picture of who your family and friends are and what they care about.

✔ **To reunite with old friends:** Thirty years after you last speak to someone, you may have a funny memory, something important to share, or just genuine curiosity about that person's whereabouts. If you keep her on your Facebook Friend List, it doesn't matter how many times you both move, change your phone numbers, or get mar-ried and change your name, you can still get in touch with each another. (If that concept scares you, Facebook also has the tools to explicitly sever connections with people you'd rather didn't find you.)

✔ **To organize groups:** You can use Facebook to organize your book club or cooking group or gather to watch sporting events and have dinner parties. Facebook Groups can add value to all these events. Creating a group on Facebook for your book club makes it easy for someone to communicate regular updates about times, dates, locations, who should bring what, and what every-one should read before attending. People can join and leave groups as they see fit, so you never have to worry about notifying those who've moved or are no longer interested in your group.

✔ **To spread the word about an event:** For one-time gather-ings, such as a Super Bowl party, Facebook Events is a great solution. All you have to do is fill out the guest list and event description — the rest takes care of itself. For the three days prior to the event, everyone receives a reminder on his Facebook Home page, so no one has an excuse for not showing up. If you want to ensure that your guest list is accurate or that people don't forget, message everyone who RSVP'd (attending or tentative, that is) or who hasn't replied. After the event is over, you can upload photos of the event. Your Super Bowl party is forever immortalized online — and everyone who RSVP'd has total access.

In the following sections, we give you the basics of how Facebook works. You can learn much, much more about Facebook in *Facebook For Dummies,* 2nd Edition, by Leah Pearlman and Carolyn Abram (Wiley).

Establishing a Profile

When you sign up for Facebook, one of the first things you do is establish your *Profile.* A Profile on Facebook is a social résumé — a page about you that you keep up-to-date with as much or as little information as you want people to know.

Facebook understands that if you were handing out résumés in the real world, you'd probably give different documents to different people. Your social résumé may have your phone number, your favorite quotes, and pictures from that crazy night in you-know-where with you-know-who. Your résumé for a potential employer would probably share your education and employment history. Your résumé for your family may include your personal address as well as show off your recent vacation photos and news about your life's changes.

You show different slices of your life and personality to different people, and a Facebook Profile, shown in Figure 4-1, allows you (no, *encourages* you) to do the same. To this end, your Profile is set up with all kinds of privacy controls to specify *who* you want to see *which* information. Many people find great value in adding to their Profile just about every piece of information they can and then unveiling each particular piece cautiously. The safest rule here is to share on your Profile any piece of information you'd share with someone in real life. The corollary applies, too: Don't share on your Profile any information that you wouldn't share with someone in real life.

Think of your Profile like a personal Web page with privacy controls for particular pieces of information. This page allows you to share, for example, your home address just with some people and your phone number with even more people. You control who sees what.

Connecting and communicating with friends

After you join Facebook, you start seeing its value by tracking down some people you know. Facebook offers the following tools to help you:

✓ **Facebook Friend Finder:** Allows you to scan the e-mail addresses in your e-mail address book to find whether those people are already on Facebook. Selectively choose among those with whom you'd like to connect.

✓ **Suggestions:** Shows you the names and pictures of people you likely know or celebrities whose news you'd like to follow. These people are selected for you based on various signals like where you live or work, or how many friends you have in common.

✓ **Search:** Helps you to find people whom you expect are already using Facebook.

After you establish a few connections, use those connections to find other people you know by searching through *their* connections for familiar names.

As Facebook grows, it becomes more likely that anyone with whom you're trying to communicate can be reached. These days it's a fairly safe assumption that you'll be able to find that person you just met at a dinner party, an old professor from college, or the childhood friend you've been meaning to catch up with.

Plus, Facebook streamlines finding and contacting people in a reliable forum. If the person you're reaching out to is active on Facebook, no matter where she lives or how many times she's changed her e-mail address, you can reach one another.

Figure 4-1: A Facebook Profile is like a social résumé.

Facebook has great tools for organizing people, information, and communication. Their utility, however, depends on you being able to reach your friends with them. The more contacts you have on Facebook, the more useful each of these tools will become for you.

Sharing your words

You have something to say. We can just tell by the look on your face. Maybe you're proud of the home team, maybe you're excited for Friday, or maybe you can't believe what you saw on the way to work this morning. All day long, things are happening to all of us that make us just want to turn to our friends and say "You know what? . . .That's what." Facebook gives you the stage and an eager audience. You can write short or long posts about the things happening around you, and distribute those posts to your friends in an easy, non-intrusive way.

Sharing your pictures

Since the invention of the modern-day camera, people have been all too eager to say "Cheese!" Photographs can make great tour guides on trips down memory lane, but only if you actually remember to develop, upload, or scrapbook them. Many memories fade away when the smiling faces are stuffed into an old shoe box, remain on undeveloped rolls of film, or are forgotten in some folder on a hard drive.

Facebook offers two great incentives for uploading, organizing, and editing your photos:

- ✓ **It provides one easy-to-access location for all your photos.** Directing any interested person to your Facebook Profile is easier than e-mailing pictures individually, sending a complicated link to a photo site, or waiting until the family reunion to show off the my-how-the-kids-have-grown pics.

- ✓ **Every photo you upload can be linked to the Profiles of the people in the photo.** For example, you upload pictures of you and your sister and link them to her Profile. Whenever someone visits her Profile, he sees those pictures; he doesn't even have to know you. This is great because it introduces longevity to photos they've never had before. As long as people are visiting your sister's Profile, they can see those pictures. Photo albums no longer have to be something people look at right after the event, and maybe then again years later.

You can still limit the visibility of any part of your Profile, including your photos, to people on your Friends List, or you can open up parts of your Profile to anyone. You can share as much or as little on your Facebook account with as many or as few people as you so desire.

LinkedIn

Your collection of friends and other contacts is known as your social network. In the past, you had no way to view other people's social networks. Now, when everyone puts their social networks on a site like LinkedIn (www.linkedin.com), you can see your friends' networks, and their friends' networks, and suddenly hidden opportunities start to become available to you.

This means you can spend more time doing research on potential opportunities (like finding a job or a new employee for your business) as well as receiving information from the larger network and not just your immediate friends. This makes the network more useful because you can literally see how you're connected with other people. And you can use these connections that LinkedIn shows you to find the second career you've always dreamed of or to connect with co-workers from years ago.

We cover the basics of LinkedIn in the following sections. For more information on putting LinkedIn to work for you, check out *LinkedIn For Dummies,* by Joel Elad, MBA (Wiley).

The different degrees of network connections

In the LinkedIn universe, the word *connection* specifically means a person who is connected to you through the site. The number of connections that you have simply means the number of people that are directly connected to you in your professional network.

Specifically, though, there are different degrees of how you're connected with people on LinkedIn:

- ✔ **First-degree connections** are people that you know personally — your past colleagues, classmates, group members, friends, family, and close associates.

- ✔ **Second-degree network members** are made up of people who know at least one member of your first-degree network connections; in other words, the friends of your friends. You can reach any of your second-degree network members by asking your first-degree connection to introduce you to his or her friend.

✔ **Third-degree network members** are made up of people who know at least one of your second-degree network members; in other words, the friends of your friends of your friends. You can reach any of your third-degree network members by asking your friend to pass along an Introduction from you to his or her friend, who then passes it to his or her friend, who is the third-degree member.

The result of this is a large chain of connections and network members, with a core of trusted friends who help you reach out and tap your friends' networks and extended networks.

What you can do with LinkedIn

After you find out about what LinkedIn is, the next step is to find out about what kinds of things you can do on LinkedIn. The following sections introduce you to the topics you need to know to get your foot in the LinkedIn door and really make the site start working for you.

Building your brand and profile

One of the best ways to think about what you can do on LinkedIn is to recognize that LinkedIn can help you build your own brand. Your name, your identity, is like a brand in terms of what people think of when they think of you. It's your professional reputation. Companies spend billions to ensure you have a certain opinion of their products, and that opinion, that perception, is their brand image. You have your own brand image in your professional life, and it's up to you to own your brand, define your brand, and push your brand.

Most people today have different online representations of their personal brand. Some people have built their own Web sites, others have created and written their own blogs, and still others have created profile pages on sites like Facebook. LinkedIn allows you to define a profile (like the one shown in Figure 4-2) and build your own brand based on your professional and educational background.

LinkedIn is *not* like Facebook. You can find some elements of similarity, but LinkedIn isn't the place to show off pictures of your grandkids.

Figure 4-2: Your LinkedIn profile page details your entire professional history.

Your LinkedIn profile can become your jumping-off point where any visitor can get a rich and detailed idea of all the skills, experiences, and interests that you bring to the table. Unlike a résumé, where you have to worry about page length and formatting, you can detail as much as you want on your LinkedIn profile, including any part-time, contract, nonprofit, and consulting work in addition to traditional professional experience. You also have other options to consider:

- ✔ Write your own summary.
- ✔ List any groups you belong to.
- ✔ Show any memberships or affiliations you have.
- ✔ Cite honors and awards you have received.
- ✔ Give and receive Recommendations from other people.
- ✔ Indicate your professional interests.
- ✔ Post Web site links to other parts of your professional identity, like a blog, a Web site, or an e-commerce store you operate.

The best part is that this is your professional identity and *you* control and shape it. You decide what the content should be. You decide what you emphasize and omit. And you decide how much of this information is visible to the world and how much is visible to your first-degree network connections.

Looking for jobs now and later

The job search is, in itself, a full-time job. Study after study shows that 60 percent to 80 percent of all jobs are found not through a job board like Monster.com, not through a newspaper classified ad, but rather by a formal or informal network of contacts where the job isn't even posted yet. LinkedIn makes it easier than ever to do some of the following tedious job-search tasks:

- **Finding the right person** at a target company, such as a hiring manager in a certain department, to discuss immediate and future job openings

- **Getting a reference** from a past boss or co-worker to use for a future job application

- **Finding information** about a company and position before the interview

- **Searching posted job listings** on a job board like LinkedIn's job board

The hidden power of LinkedIn is that it helps you find jobs you weren't looking for or applying to directly. This is when you're a *passive job seeker,* currently employed but interested in the right opportunity. Currently, over 130,000 recruiters are members of LinkedIn, constantly using the search functions to go through the database and find skilled members that match their job-search requirements.

Finding out all kinds of valuable information

You can use LinkedIn to find out more than just information about your job search. You can use this immense database of professionals to find out what skills seem to be the most popular within a certain industry and job title. You can learn how many project managers live within 50 miles of you. You can really learn more by finding past employees of a company and interviewing them about their previous job. LinkedIn now has thousands of detailed Company Profiles that not only show company statistics, but recent hires, promotions, changes, and lists of employees who are closely connected with you.

Imagine if you could pick the brains of tens of millions of professionals around the world about almost any topic. Well, now you can, using a system called LinkedIn Answers. With LinkedIn Answers, you can post a question about a certain topic, mostly business- or LinkedIn-related. Other LinkedIn members can browse the questions and write up free responses — from the one-line response to the three-page essay — to share their thoughts and answer your question the best they can. There's no think-tank to pay, no pre-qualifications or lag time in your data gathering. Typically, you start to see people responding within one to two business days.

Best of all, LinkedIn can help you find specific information on a variety of topics. You can do a search to find out the interests of your next sales prospect, the name of a former employee you can talk to about a company you like, or how you can join a start-up in your target industry by reaching out to the co-founder. You can sit back and skim the news, or you can dive in and hunt for the right facts. It all depends on what method best fits your goals.

Expanding your network

You have your network today, but what about the future? Whether you want to move up in your industry, look for a new job, start your own company, or achieve some other goal, one way to achieve these goals is to expand your network. LinkedIn provides a fertile ground to reach like-minded and well-connected professionals who share a common interest, experience, or group membership. The site also provides several online mechanisms to reduce the friction of communication, so you can spend more time building your network instead of searching for the right person.

First and foremost, LinkedIn lets you identify and contact members of other people's professional networks, and best of all, you don't have to contact them via a cold call, but with your friend's Recommendation or Introduction. In addition, you can find out more about your new contact before you send the first message, so you don't have to waste time figuring out whether this is someone who could be beneficial to have in your network.

You can also meet new people through various groups on LinkedIn, whether it's an alumni group from your old school, a group of past employees from the same company, or a group of people interested in improving their public-speaking skills. LinkedIn Groups are ways for you to identify with other like-minded members, search for specific group members, and share information about the Group with each other.

Twitter

Twitter is a fast-evolving, surprisingly powerful way to exchange ideas and information and stay in touch with people, businesses, and organizations that you care about. It's a social network — a kind of map of who you know and who you're interested in (whether you know them personally or not).

Twitter has one central feature: It lets users instantly post entries of 140 characters or less, known as *tweets,* online through www.twitter.com or your cellphone. Your tweets are generally published to the world at large where anyone can read them on Twitter.com (unless you set up a private account, so that only those you choose can see your tweets).

Think you can't say anything meaningful in 140 characters? Think again. Not only are *twitterers* (people who use Twitter) innovating clever forms of one-liners, haiku, quotes, and humor, but they're including links — in 23 percent of all tweets by one measure — and links carry a lot more information and context.

The idea of Twitter sounds simple — even a little too simple. But when you think that millions of people around the world are posting Twitter messages, following other people's Twitter streams, and responding to one another, you can start to see the significance behind Twitter's appeal. True, Twitter can look like it's full of noise. But as soon as you find interesting people and accounts to follow, your Twitter stream (shown in Figure 4-3) shifts from a cascade of disjointed chatter to one of the most versatile, useful online communications tools yet seen — that is, if you take the time to learn to use that tool correctly.

We cover the basics of Twitter in the following sections. For more information on Twitter — much more than we have space for here — check out *Twitter For Dummies,* by Laura Fitton, Michael Gruen, and Leslie Poston (Wiley).

Figure 4-3: Your Twitter stream contains all the tweets of all the people you follow.

Understanding who uses Twitter and why

All different kinds of people use Twitter for different reasons. You can use Twitter to follow your friends and family and keep updated on what they're doing, as well as to share with them what you're up to. You can follow your favorite authors or athletes or journalists on Twitter, and be kept apprised of their latest projects. You can follow the organizations you support and the businesses you frequent, to learn about events and sales and other opportunities.

How individuals use Twitter

Looking at Twitter for the first time, you might be compelled to ask, "But *why* are all these people, many of whom seem like just random strangers, talking?" At first glance, Twitter seems flooded with disjointed conversations, interactions, and information. You can find news headlines, political debates, observations on the weather, and requests for advice. The idea of Twitter can be a bit confusing for new twitterers.

People have many reasons for using Twitter:

- ✔ **To connect:** Most people start using Twitter to forge connections and be a part of a community. Others just want to be heard. Twitter lets millions of people around the world hear what you have to say; then it lets you connect with the ones who want to hear from or talk to you about your passions, interests, and ideas.

- ✔ **To record:** Some people tweet as a way to take notes on life. They use Twitter at conferences, events, or just walking around and may even jog their own memories later about something that happened or what they've discovered. For example, if you're walking down the street and you notice a new restaurant you want to check out when you have more time, you might tweet about that. Now everyone who follows you knows about this interesting-looking place, and you have a way of remembering to go back there yourself.

- ✔ **To share:** Some people use Twitter to share what they think, read, and know. They may tweet links to great articles or interesting items, or they may tweet original thoughts, ideas, hints, and tricks. Some tweet notes from speeches or classes, and others share choice bits of their inner monologue. Even when this information can get pretty obscure, with millions of listeners, someone's bound to find it informative or interesting.

- ✔ **To stay in touch:** Whole families and groups of long-term friends use Twitter to stay in touch. Twitter can send public or private notes to your friends, and it stores all sent messages.

How organizations use Twitter

The power of Twitter works for organizations large and small. You can follow the organizations you support, and keep up on their progress.

Groups such as churches and local charities can use Twitter to provide an additional way for members to connect, plan, and reach out beyond their immediate community. Preachers tweet about their planned sermons, youth group directors tweet about events, and local soup kitchens tweet when they need help. Whether it's extra hands for a project, far-reaching assistance with a fundraiser, or some other big idea, Twitter can enable organizations operating on a budget to think on their feet.

But Twitter isn't just for charities. Enthusiasts of just about any interest have banded together on Twitter. For example, you can find organizations for food and wine lovers, sharing recipes and swapping restaurant reviews on Twitter. (You can search for the subjects that interest you at http://search. twitter.com.)

Twitter has also been a big help for community efforts. Whether it's Amber Alerts, fundraisers, searching for kidney donors, or rescuing James Buck from an Egyptian jail (http://twitter. com/jamesbuck/statuses/786571964), Twitter has shone as a tool for social good. Plenty of people in the world want to lend a helping hand, and Twitter's platform makes it easy, in real time, with a global network of connections.

You can follow the organizations you support, and keep up on their progress.

How businesses use Twitter

If individuals, community groups, and nonprofit groups, can use Twitter (as we discuss in the preceding sections), businesses can use it, too.

For example, discount airline JetBlue uses Twitter to advertise fare specials, put out weather alerts, and conduct customer service (http://twitter.com/JetBlue). Coffee retailer Starbucks uses Twitter to connect with customers and spread company culture (http://twitter.com/Starbucks), as does online shoe retailer Zappos.com (http://twitter. com/zappos).

You can follow the businesses you frequent and take advantage of the deals they offer.

Getting your tweet wet

When you log into Twitter, a question appears in large print across the top of the screen: "What are you doing?" The most basic activity on Twitter is to answer that question, whenever and however you feel like it. The beauty of this simple question is that you can answer it in so many different ways, and your answer can spark so many conversations.

While you get more comfortable using Twitter, you may find that you ignore the question of "What are you doing?" altogether. That's okay. Twitter is inherently flexible and open-ended, so you don't need to stick to a rigid set of rules. In effect, Twitter is what you make it.

The "What are you doing?" prompt can get some new Twitter users stuck in a rut. Sometimes, twitterers freeze up out of self-consciousness, concern that they're not doing it right, or just plain old 140-character writer's block. You know these Twitter accounts when you see them: The twitterers end up twittering only about what they had for breakfast, that they're leaving the office to go home and watch their favorite TV show, or various other mundane life updates that don't spark much conversation. Many of these Twitter users don't end up getting involved in the Twitter culture, and some then stop using Twitter altogether.

You can get much more value from Twitter — and have a lot more fun — if you just let yourself relax and talk about what's on your mind. Passionate about aardvarks? Send out a few tweets with aardvark facts and see who talks back to you. Have a burning desire to change careers from accounting to roadie for a rock band? Talk about it! You can probably get a response or two.

Be sure to let your friends and family know you're on Twitter. You can put your Twitter address (`http://twitter.com/`*yourname*) at the bottom of your e-mail messages to let people know they can follow you there. And if they're scratching their heads wondering why they would want to join Twitter in the first place, have them go to `http://bit.ly/270tIV` and watch a little video on what Twitter is.